Devoutly I Adore Thee

The Prayers and Hymns
of St. Thomas Aquinas

St. Thomas Aquinas

Devoutly I Adore Thee

The Prayers and Hymns
of St. Thomas Aquinas

Translated and edited by
Robert Anderson
and
Johann Moser

SOPHIA INSTITUTE PRESS
Manchester, New Hampshire

With two exceptions, the Latin texts for these prayers and hymns are from the Marietti edition (1954) of St. Thomas Aquinas's *Opuscula theologica* II, pp. 275-289. The seventeenth stanza of "Lauda, Sion, Salvatorem" is from the Vivès edition (1876), vol. 29, p. 343, because it was omitted from the Marietti edition. "In Articulo Mortis" is from p. 379 of the *Fontes Vitae Sancti Thomae*, D. Prümmer and M. H. Laurent, which appeared serially in *Revue thomiste* from 1912-1934. The text for the prayers and hymns has been emended where obviously flawed. Spelling has been standardized and punctuation conformed to contemporary conventions.

Sophia Institute Press
Box 5284, Manchester, NH 03108
1-800-888-9344

Library of Congress Cataloging-in-Publication Data

Thomas, Aquinas, Saint, 1225?-1274.

[Selections. English & Latin. 1993]

Devoutly I adore thee : the prayers and hymns of St. Thomas Aquinas /
St. Thomas Aquinas ; translated and edited by Robert Anderson and Johann Moser.

p. cm.

Parallel text in English and Latin.

Includes bibliographical references.

ISBN 0-918477-19-0 (hardcover)

1. Prayers, Medieval. 2. Hymns, Latin—Texts. 3. Hymns, Latin—Texts—Translations into English. I. Anderson, Robert, 1961- . II. Moser, Johann, 1940- . III. Title.

BX890.T62E6 1993

242' .802—dc20   93-37487 CIP

2 4 6 8 10 9 7 5 3 1

TABLE OF CONTENTS

Prayers

Prayers during the Sacrifice of the Mass

Hymns from the
Office of the Feast of Corpus Christi

A Last Prayer

Biographical Note

Devoutly I Adore Thee

*The Prayers and Hymns
of St. Thomas Aquinas*

We do not pray to change divine decree, but only to obtain what God has decided will be obtained through prayer.

In other words, as St. Gregory says, "by asking, men deserve to receive what the all-powerful God has decreed from all eternity to give them."

St. Thomas Aquinas
Summa theologiae
II, II, Q. 83, Art. 2

Prayers

Ad Vitam Sapienter Instituendam

Quam Angelicus quotidie recitare solebat
ante imaginem Christi.

Concede mihi, misericors Deus,
 quae tibi sunt placita,
  ardenter concupiscere,
  prudenter investigare,
  veraciter agnoscere,
  et perfecte adimplere,
   ad laudem et gloriam nominis tui.

Ordina, Deus meus, statum meum.

Et quod a me requiris ut faciam,
 tribue ut sciam.

Et da exsequi,
 sicut oportet
  et expedit animae meae.

Da mihi, Domine Deus meus,
 inter prospera et adversa
  non deficere,

For Ordering a Life Wisely

St. Thomas recited this daily before the image of Christ.

O merciful God, grant that I may
        desire ardently,
        search prudently,
        recognize truly,
        and bring to perfect completion
    whatever is pleasing to You
        for the praise and glory of Your name.

Put my life in good order, O my God.

Grant that I may know
    what You require me to do.

Bestow upon me
    the power to accomplish Your will,
        as is necessary and fitting
           for the salvation of my soul.

Grant to me, O Lord my God,
    that I may not falter in times
        of prosperity or adversity,

ut in illis non extollar
et in istis non deprimar.

De nullo gaudeam
vel doleam,
nisi quod ducat ad te
vel abducat a te.

Nulli placere appetam
vel displicere timeam,
nisi tibi.

Vilescant mihi, Domine,
omnia transitoria,
et cara mihi sint
omnia aeterna.

Taedeat me gaudii
quod est sine te,
nec aliud cupiam
quod est extra te.

so that I may not be exalted in the former,
     nor dejected in the latter.

May I not rejoice in anything
     unless it leads me to You;
may I not be saddened by anything
     unless it turns me from You.

May I desire to please no one,
     nor fear to displease anyone,
     but You.

May all transitory things, O Lord,
     be worthless to me
and may all things eternal
     be ever cherished by me.

May any joy without You
     be burdensome for me
and may I not desire anything else
     besides You.

Delectet me, Domine, labor,
>> qui est pro te,
> et taediosa sit mihi omnis quies
>> quae est sine te.

Da mihi, Deus meus,
>> cor meum ad te dirigere
>> et in defectione mea
>>> cum emendationis proposito
>>>> constanter dolere.

Fac me, Domine Deus meus,
>> obedientem sine contradictione,
>> pauperem sine dejectione,
>> castum sine corruptione,
>> patientem sine murmuratione,
>> humilem sine fictione,
>> hilarem sine dissolutione,
>> maturum sine gravedine,
>> agilem sine levitate,
>> timentem te sine desperatione,
>> veracem sine duplicitate,
>> operantem bona sine praesumptione,

May all work, O Lord,
     delight me when done for Your sake
   and may all repose not centered in You
     be ever wearisome for me.

Grant unto me, my God,
     that I may direct my heart to You
     and that in my failures
       I may ever feel remorse for my sins
         and never lose the resolve to change.

O Lord my God, make me
     submissive without protest,
     poor without discouragement,
     chaste without regret,
     patient without complaint,
     humble without posturing,
     cheerful without frivolity,
     mature without gloom,
     and quick-witted without flippancy.

O Lord my God, let me
     fear You without losing hope,
     be truthful without guile,
     do good works without presumption,

proximum corripere sine elatione,
 ipsum aedificare verbo
et exemplo sine simulatione.

Da mihi, Domine Deus,
 cor pervigil,
  quod nulla abducat a te
   curiosa cogitatio.

Da nobile,
 quod nulla deorsum trahat
  indigna affectio.

Da rectum,
 quod nulla seorsum obliquet
  sinistra intentio.

Da firmum,
 quod nulla frangat tribulatio.

Da liberum,
 quod nulla sibi vindicet
  violenta affectio.

rebuke my neighbor without haughtiness,
and — without hypocrisy —
strengthen him by word and example.

Give to me, O Lord God,
a watchful heart,
which no capricious thought
can lure away from You.

Give to me
a noble heart,
which no unworthy desire can debase.

Give to me
a resolute heart,
which no evil intention can divert.

Give to me
a stalwart heart,
which no tribulation can overcome.

Give to me
a temperate heart,
which no violent passion can enslave.

Largire mihi, Domine Deus meus,
> intellectum te cognoscentem,
> diligentiam te quaerentem,
> sapientiam te invenientem,
> conversationem tibi placentem,
> perseverantiam fidenter te expectantem,
> et fiduciam te finaliter amplectentem.

Da tuis poenis
> hic affligi per poenitentiam,
>> tuis beneficiis
> in via uti per gratiam,
>> tuis gaudiis
> in patria perfrui per gloriam.

Qui vivis et regnas, Deus,
> per omnia saecula saeculorum.

Amen

Give to me, O Lord my God,
      understanding of You,
      diligence in seeking You,
      wisdom in finding You,
      discourse ever pleasing to You,
      perseverance in waiting for You,
      and confidence in finally embracing You.

Grant that
      as penance
          I may be afflicted by Your hardships now,
      through grace
          I may rely on Your blessings on the way,
      and in glory
          I may enjoy You fully
               in the Kingdom of Heaven.

You Who live and reign,
      God, world without end.

Amen

Pro Dei Beneficiis

Laudo, glorifico, benedico te, Deus meus,
    propter immensa
    indigno mihi praestita beneficia.

Laudo
        clementiam tuam
            me diu expectantem,
        dulcedinem tuam
            ulcisci simulantem,

        pietatem tuam
            vocantem,
        benignitatem
            suscipientem,
        misericordiam
            peccata remittentem.

        bonitatem
            supra merita impendentem,

For God's Blessing

I praise, glorify, and bless You, my God
      for the immeasurable blessings
      shown to me who am unworthy of them.

I praise
      Your compassion
            extended to me for so long a time
      and Your gentleness
            appearing often in the guise of correction.

I praise
      Your tenderness
            calling out to me,
      Your kindness
            that sustains me,
      and Your mercy
            for the forgiveness of my sins.

I praise
      Your goodness
            given to me beyond what I deserve

patientiam
    injuriae non recordantem,

humilitatem
    consolantem,
patientiam
    protegentem,
aeternitatem
    conservantem,
veritatem
    remunerantem.

Quid dicam, Deus meus,
    de tua ineffabili largitate?

Tu enim vocas fugientem.
Suscipis revertentem.
Adjuvas titubantem.
Laetificas desperantem.
Stimulas negligentem.
Armas pugnantem.
Coronas triumphantem.
Peccatorem post poenitentiam
        non spernis.
Et injuriae non memineris.

and Your forbearance
        that does not remember grievances.

I praise
        Your humility
                that consoles me,
        Your patience
                that shelters me,
        Your eternity
                that preserves me,
        and Your truth
                that rewards me.

What can I proclaim, my God,
        about Your ineffable generosity?

        For You call the fugitive back.
        You welcome the one who returns.
        You sustain the faltering.
        You gladden the despondent.
        You prod the negligent.
        You arm the warrior.
        You crown the victor.
        You spurn not the repentant sinner.
        You do not remember his wrongdoing.

A multis liberas periculis.
Ad poenitentiam cor emollis.
Terres suppliciis.
Allicis promissis.
Castigas flagellis.
Angelico ministerio custodis.

Ministras temporalia.
Reservas nobis aeterna.
Hortaris dignitate creationis.
Invitas clementia redemptionis.
Promittis praemia remunerationis.

Pro quibus omnibus laudes referre non sufficio.

Majestati tuae gratias ago
        propter immensae bonitatis tuae abundantiam,
ut semper in me gratiam multiplices,
        et multiplicatam conserves,
        et conservatam remuneres.

Amen

You free him from many perils.
You soften his heart for penitence.
You frighten him with chastisement.
You entice him with promises.
You castigate him with rods.
You guard him with ministering angels.

For You supply us with all temporal goods.
You reserve for us an eternal good.
You inspire us with the beauty of creation.
You appeal to us with the mercy of redemption.
You promise us blessings in reward.

For all these I am incapable of sufficient praise.

I thank Your majesty
  for the abundance of Your immense goodness.
May You always increase Your grace in me,
  preserve that increase,
    and reward what You have preserved.

Amen

Ad Beatissimam Virginem Mariam

O beatissima et dulcissima Virgo Maria,
>Mater Dei, omni pietate plenissima,
>summi Regis filia,
>Domina Angelorum,
>Mater omnium credentium,

in sinum pietatis tuae
  commendo hodie
  et omnibus diebus vitae meae
>corpus meum et animam meam,
>omnesque actus meos, cogitationes, volitiones,
>desideria, locutiones, operationes,
>omnemque vitam, finemque meum,

ut per tua suffragia
>disponantur in bonum
>>secundum voluntatem dilecti Filii tui
>>>Domini nostri Jesu Christi,

ut sis mihi,
>O Domina mea sanctissima,

To the Most Blessed Virgin Mary

O most blessed and sweet Virgin Mary,
  Mother of God, filled with all tenderness,
  Daughter of the most high King,
  Lady of the angels,
  Mother of all the faithful,

On this day and all the days of my life,
  I entrust to your merciful heart
    my body and my soul,
    all my acts, thoughts, choices,
    desires, words, deeds,
    my entire life and death,

So that, with your assistance,
  all may be ordered to the good
    according to the will of your beloved Son,
      our Lord Jesus Christ.

Be to me,
  my most holy Lady,

adjutrix et consolatrix
      contra insidias et laqueos
            hostis antiqui
            et omnium inimicorum meorum.

A dilecto Filio tuo
      Domino nostro Jesu Christo
   mihi impetrare digneris gratiam,
       cum qua potenter resistere valeam
        tentationibus
            mundi, carnis, et daemonis,
ac semper habere firmum propositum
        ulterius non peccandi,
          sed in tuo et dilecti Filii tui
            servitio perseverandi.

Deprecor te etiam,
  Domina mea sanctissima,
       ut impetres mihi veram obedientiam
         et veram cordis humilitatem,

ut veraciter me agnoscam
      miserum, ac fragilem peccatorem,

a comforter
and an ally against the stratagems
and traps of the ancient enemy
and of all those
who harbor ill intentions against me.

From your beloved Son,
our Lord Jesus Christ,
request for me
the grace to resist firmly
the temptations
of the world, the flesh, and the devil,
and a constant resolve
to sin no more
and to persevere in your service
and the service of your beloved Son.

My most holy Lady,
I also beseech you to obtain for me
true obedience and true humility of heart

So that I may recognize myself truly
as a sinner — wretched and weak —

et impotentem,
> non solum ad faciendum
> quodcumque opus bonum,
> sed etiam ad resistendum
>> continuis impugnationibus,
> sine gratia et adjutorio Creatoris mei
> et sanctis precibus tuis.

Impetra mihi etiam,
> O Domina mea dulcissima,
>> perpetuam mentis et corporis castitatem,
> ut puro corde et casto corpore
>> dilecto Filio tui et tibi
>>> in tuo ordine
>>>> valeam deservire.

Obtine mihi ab eo
> voluntariam paupertatem
>> cum patientia
>>> et mentis tranquillitate,
>> ut labores ejusdem ordinis
>>> valeam sustinere
>> et pro salute propria et proximorum
>>> valeam laborare.

and powerless,
>without the grace and help of my Creator
>and without your holy prayers,
to do any kind of good work
or even to resist
>the unrelenting assaults of evil.

Procure for me also,
>O my most sweet Lady,
>>perpetual purity of mind and body,
so that with a pure heart and chaste body
>I may be strengthened
>>to serve you and your beloved Son
>>>through the Dominican Order.

From Him,
>obtain for me a spirit of poverty
>>willingly accepted
>>>with patience and tranquillity of mind,
>so that I will have the strength
>>to sustain the labors of this Order
>>and to work for my own salvation
>>>and that of my neighbors.

Impetra mihi etiam,
  O dulcissima Domina,
    caritatem veram,
      qua sacratissimum Filium tuum
        Dominum nostrum
        Jesum Christum
    toto corde diligam
    et te post ipsum super omnia
    et proximum
      in Deo et propter Deum.

Sicque
    de bono ejus gaudeam,
    de malo doleam,
    nullumque contemnam,
    neque temerarie judicem,
    neque in corde meo alicui me praeponam.

Fac etiam, O Regina caeli,
    ut dulcissimi Filii tui timorem pariter
      et amorem semper
        in corde meo habeam;

Obtain for me as well,
  O most sweet Lady,
      true charity with which
         from the depths of my heart
      I may love
         your most holy Son, our Lord Jesus Christ,
         and, after Him,
      love you above all other things,
       and love my neighbor
         in God and because of God.

Thereby may I
      rejoice in his goodness,
      sorrow over his evils,
      despise no one,
      never judge rashly,
      and never in my heart exalt myself over anyone.

Grant, O Queen of Heaven,
      that ever in my heart
         I may have fear and love alike
            for your most sweet Son;

et de tantis beneficiis mihi,
    non meis meritis,
        sed ipsius benignitate collatis
        semper gratiam agam;

ac de peccatis meis
    puram et sinceram confessionem
    et veram poenitentiam faciam,
        ut suam consequi merear
            misericordiam et gratiam.

Oro etiam, ut in fine vitae meae
  tu,
    Mater unica,
    caeli porta,
    et peccatorum advocata,
        me indignum servum tuum
            a sancta fide catholica
            deviare non permittas;

sed tua magna pietate et misericordia
    mihi succurras,
    et a malis spiritibus me defendas;

That I may always give thanks
>> for the many blessings bestowed upon me
>>> not for my merits
>>> but by His kindness;

And that I may ever
>> make a pure and sincere confession
>> and do true penance for my sins,
>>> in order that I might deserve
>>>> to obtain His mercy and grace.

I pray also that, at the end of my life,
> you,
>> Mother without compare,
>> Gate of Heaven,
>> and Advocate of sinners,
>>> will not allow me, your unworthy servant,
>>>> to stray from the holy Catholic faith

But that you will
>> protect me with your great piety and mercy,
>> defend me from evil spirits,

ac in benedicta Filii tui gloriosa passione
et in tua propria intercessione
spe accepta,
veniam de peccatis meis ab eo
mihi impetres;

atque me in tua et ejus dilectione
morientem
in viam salvationis et salutis dirigas.

Amen

and obtain for me,
   through the blessed and glorious Passion of your Son
      and through your own intercession,
            received in hope,
         the forgiveness of all of my sins.

When I die in your love and His love,
   may you direct me
      into the way of salvation and blessedness.

               Amen

Pro Obtinendis Virtutibus

O Deus

     omnipotens, omnia sciens,

     principio et fine carens,

qui es virtutum

     donator,

     et conservator,

     et remunerator,

digneris me

     stabilire solido fidei fundamento,

     et tueri inexpugnabili spei clipeo,

     atque decorare nuptiali caritatis vestimento.

Da mihi

     per justitiam

         tibi subesse,

     per prudentiam

         insidias diaboli cavere,

     per temperantiam

         medium tenere,

To Acquire the Virtues

O God,
    all-powerful and all-knowing,
    without beginning and without end,
You Who are
    the source,
    the sustainer,
    and the rewarder of all virtues,

Grant that I may
    abide on the firm ground of faith,
    be sheltered by an impregnable shield of hope,
    and be adorned in the bridal garment of charity.

Grant that I may
    through justice
        be subject to You,
    through prudence
        avoid the beguilements of the devil,
    through temperance
        exercise restraint,

per fortitudinem
    adversa patienter tolerare.

Da
    bonum quod habeo,
        non habentibus
            libenter impertiri;
    bonum quod non habeo,
        ab habentibus
            humiliter quaerere;

malum culpae
    quod feci,
        veraciter accusare;
malum poenae
    quod sustineo,
        aequanimiter ferre;

bono proximi non invidere;
    de bonis tuis semper gratias agere;

and through fortitude
    endure adversity with patience.

Grant that
    whatever good things I have,
        I may share generously
            with those who have not
    and that
        whatever good things I do not have,
            I may request humbly
                from those who do.

Grant that I may
    judge rightly
        the evil of the wrongs I have done
    and bear calmly
        the punishments
            I have brought upon myself,

and that I may
    never envy my neighbor's possessions
    and ever give thanks for Your good things.

habitu,
incessu,
et motu
disciplinam semper servare;
linguam a vaniloquio restringere;
pedes a discursu cohibere;
oculos a vago visu comprimere;
aures a rumoribus separare;
vultum humiliter inclinare;
mentem in caelestia levare;
transitoria contemnere;
te tantummodo desiderare;

carnem domare;
conscientiam expurgare;
sanctos honorare;
te digne laudare;
in bono proficere;
et bonos actus fine sancto terminare.

Planta in me, Domine, virtutes,
ut circa divina
sim devotus,
circa humana officia
providus,

Grant that I may always observe modesty
             in the way I dress,
             the way I walk,
             and the gestures I use,
        restrain my tongue from frivolous talk,
        prevent my feet from leading me astray,
        keep my eyes from wandering glances,
        shelter my ears from rumors,
        lower my gaze in humility,
        lift my mind to thoughts of heaven,
        contemn all that will pass away,
        and love You only.

Grant that I may subdue my flesh
        and cleanse my conscience,
        honor the saints and praise You worthily,
        advance in goodness,
        and end a life of good works with a holy death.

Plant deep in me, Lord, all the virtues,
        that I might be
             devout in divine matters,
             discerning in human affairs,

circa usum proprii corporis
nulli onerosus.

Da mihi, Domine,
ferventem contritionem,
puram confessionem,
perfectam satisfactionem.

Ordinare me digneris interius per bonam vitam,
ut faciam
quod deceat
et quod mihi proficiat
ad meritum
et reliquis proximis ad exemplum.

Da mihi, ut nunquam ea
quae fiunt insipienter appetam
et quae fiunt acediose fastidiam,

ne contingat inchoanda ante tempus appetere
aut inchoata ante consummationem deserere.

Amen

and burdensome to no one
    in fulfilling my own bodily needs.

Grant to me, Lord,
    fervent contrition,
    pure confession,
    and complete reparation.

Order me inwardly through a good life,
    that I might do
    what is right
    and what will be
      meritorious for me
      and a good example for others.

Grant that I may
    always restrain my foolish impulses,
    yet never succumb to lethargy,

Lest I begin things before I should
    or abandon them before finishing.

Amen

Ante Studium

Quam frequenter dicebat
antequam dictaret, scriberet, aut praedicaret.

Creator ineffabilis,
   qui de thesauris sapientiae tuae
         tres Angelorum hierarchias designasti,
               et eas super caelum empyreum
         miro ordine collocasti,
         atque universi partes
                     elegantissime disposuisti,

tu inquam qui
            verus fons
            luminis et sapientiae diceris
                  atque supereminens principium

infundere digneris
            super intellectus mei tenebras
                     tuae radium claritatis,
            duplices in quibus natus sum
                  a me removens tenebras,
                     peccatum scilicet et ignorantiam.

Before Study

*St. Thomas frequently recited this
before he dictated, wrote, or preached.*

Ineffable Creator,
  Who, from the treasures of Your wisdom,
      has established three hierarchies of angels,
      has arrayed them in marvelous order
          above the fiery heavens,
      and has marshaled the regions
              of the universe with such artful skill,

You are proclaimed
        the true font of light and wisdom,
        and the primal origin
            raised high beyond all things.

Pour forth a ray of Your brightness
          into the darkened places of my mind;
    disperse from my soul
          the twofold darkness
              into which I was born:
                  sin and ignorance.

Tu, qui linguas infantium facis disertas,
      linguam meam erudias
      atque in labiis meis gratiam
            tuae benedictionis infundas.

Da mihi
      intelligendi acumen,
      retinendi capacitatem,
      addiscendi modum et facilitatem,
      interpretandi subtilitatem,
      loquendi gratiam copiosam.

Ingressum instruas,
      progressum dirigas,
         egressum compleas.

Tu qui es verus Deus et homo,
      qui vivis et regnas in saecula saeculorum.

Amen

You make eloquent the tongues of infants.
>   Refine my speech
>   and pour forth upon my lips
>   the goodness of Your blessing.

Grant to me
>   keenness of mind,
>   capacity to remember,
>   skill in learning,
>   subtlety to interpret,
>   and eloquence in speech.

May You
>   guide the beginning of my work,
>   direct its progress,
>   and bring it to completion.

You Who are true God and true Man,
>   Who live and reign, world without end.

Amen

Pro Peccatorum Remissione

Ad te fontem misericordiae, Deus,
      accedo peccator.
Ergo digneris me lavare immundum.

O sol justitiae,
      illumina caecum.
O aeterne medice,
      cura vulneratum.
O Rex regum,
      indue spoliatum.
O mediator Dei et hominum,
      reconcilia reum.
O pastor bone,
      reduc errantem.

Da, Deus,
      misericordiam misero,
      indulgentiam criminoso,
      vitam mortuo,
      justificationem impio,
      unctionem gratiae indurato.

For the Forgiveness of Sins

To You, O God, Fountain of Mercy,
    I come, a sinner.
May You wash away my impurity.

O Sun of Justice,
    give sight to the blind.
O Eternal Healer,
    cure the wounded.
O King of Kings,
    restore the despoiled.
O Mediator of God and man,
    reconcile the sinful.
O Good Shepherd,
    lead back the straying.
O God,
    have pity on the wretched,
    show leniency to the guilty,
    bestow life on the dead,
    reform the impious,
    and give the balm of grace
        to the hard of heart.

O clementissime,
      revoca fugientem,
      trahe resistentem,
      erige cadentem,
      tene stantem,
      conduc ambulantem.

Ne obliviscaris te obliviscentem.
Ne deseras te deserentem.
Ne despicias peccantem.

Ego enim peccando
      te, Deum meum, offendi,
      proximum laesi,
      mihi non peperci.

Peccavi, Deus meus,
      fragilitate contra te,
         Patrem omnipotentem,
      ignorantia contra te,
         Filium sapientem,
      malitia contra te,
         Spiritum Sanctum clementem.

O most merciful God,
>   call back the one who flees,
>   draw back the one who resists,
>   lift up the one who falls,
>   support the one who stands,
>   and accompany the one who walks.

Do not forget those who forget You.
Do not desert those who desert You.
Do not despise those who sin against You.

For in sinning,
>   I have offended You, my God;
>   I have harmed my neighbor;
>   I have not even spared myself injury.

I have sinned, O my God,
>   against You, almighty Father,
>   because of my weakness;
>   against You, all-knowing Son,
>   because of my ignorance;
>   against You, merciful Holy Spirit,
>   because of my malice.

Et his offendi te
    Trinitatem excellentem.

Heu mihi misero!
    Quot
    et quanta commisi.
    Qualia perpetravi.

Dereliqui te, Domine.
    De bonitate tua conqueror,
        amore malo accedente,
        timore malo humiliante,

quibus potius
    te amittere
        quam amatis carere,
    potius te offendere
        quam timenda non incurrere volui.

O Deus meus,
    quantum nocui
        verbo et opere,
        peccando
            latenter, patenter, et contumaciter.

Thus have I offended You,
    most high Trinity.

Woe to me, a pitiful soul!
    How many,
    how great,
    and how diverse
        are the sins I have committed.

I abandoned You, Lord.
    I questioned Your goodness,
        yielding to evil cravings
        and weakening myself with harmful fears.

By such things, I preferred
    to lose You
        rather than abandon what I desired,
    to offend You
        rather than face what ought not to be feared.

O my God,
    how much harm have I done
        by word and deed,
        and by sinning
            secretly, openly, and defiantly.

Quare
    pro mea fragilitate supplico,
        ut non attendas meam iniquitatem
            sed tuam immensam bonitatem,

et remittas clementer
    quae feci,
        donans
            dolorem pro praeteritis
            et cautelam efficacem de futuris.

Amen

Therefore,
   out of my weakness I beg You
      not to attend to my iniquity,
         but rather to Your immense goodness.

And I beg you mercifully to pardon
      what I have done,
         granting me
            sorrow for my past actions
            and precaution in the future.

Amen

Qua Ad Caelum Adspirat

Quam ipse intime contemplans dicebat

Te Deum totius consolationis
    invoco,
        qui nihil in nobis
praeter tua dona cernis,
      ut mihi post hujus vitae terminum
        donare digneris
           cognitionem primae veritatis,
           fruitionem divinae majestatis.

Da etiam corpori meo, largissime remunerator,
    claritatis pulchritudinem,
    agilitatis promptitudinem,
    subtilitatis aptitudinem,
    impassibilitatis fortitudinem.

Apponas istis
    affluentiam divitiarum,
    influentiam deliciarum,
    confluentiam bonorum,

For the Attainment of Heaven

St. Thomas often prayed these lines while contemplating.

God of all consolation,
>> You Who see nothing in us
>>> but what You have given us,
I invoke Your help:
>> after this life has run its course,
>>> grant me
>>>> knowledge of You, the first Truth,
>>>> and enjoyment of Your divine majesty.

O most bountiful Rewarder, endow my body
>> with the splendor of a beautiful soul,
>> with swift responsiveness to all commands,
>> with complete subservience to the spirit,
>> and with freedom from all vulnerability.

Add to these
>> an abundance of Your riches,
>> a river of delights,
>> and a flood of other goods

ut gaudere possim
      supra me de tua consolatione,
      infra de loci amoenitate,
      intra de corporis et animae glorificatione,
      juxta de Angelorum et hominum
          delectabili associatione.

Consequatur apud te, clementissime Pater,
      mea rationalis potentia
          sapientiae illustrationem,
      concupiscibilis
          desiderabilium adeptionem,
      irascibilis
          triumphi laudem,

ubi est, apud te,
      evasio periculorum,
      distinctio mansionum,
      concordia voluntatum,

ubi est
      amoenitas vernalis,
      luciditas aestivalis,
      ubertas autumnalis,
      et requies hiemalis.

So that I may enjoy
> Your solace above me,
> a delightful garden beneath my feet,
> the glorification of body and soul within me,
> and the sweet companionship
>> of men and angels around me.

With You, most merciful Father,
> may my mind attain
>> the enlightenment of wisdom,
> my desire
>> what is truly desirable,
> and my courage
>> the praise of triumph.

There, with You, is
> refuge from all dangers,
> multitude of dwelling places,
> and harmony of wills.

There, with You, resides
> the cheerfulness of spring,
> the brilliance of summer,
> the fruitfulness of autumn,
> and the gentle repose of winter.

Da, Domine Deus,
vitam sine morte,
gaudium sine dolore,
ubi est summa libertas,
libera securitas,
secura tranquillitas,
jucunda felicitas,
felix aeternitas,
aeterna beatitudo,
veritatis visio,
atque laudatio, Deus.

Amen

Give me, O Lord my God,
        that life without death
        and that joy without sorrow
   where there is
        the greatest freedom,
        unconfined security,
        secure tranquillity,
        delightful happiness,
        happy eternity,
        eternal blessedness,
        the vision of truth,
        and praise, O God.

Amen

Prayers
during the
Sacrifice of the Mass

Ad Sacrosanctum Sacramentum

O sacrum convivium
>in quo Christus sumitur,
>recolitur memoria Passionis ejus,
>mens impletur gratia,
>et futurae gloriae nobis pignus datur.

O quam sauvis est, Domine, spiritus tuus,
>qui ut dulcedinem tuam in filios demonstrares,
>pane suavissimo de caelo praestito,
>esurientes reples bonis,
>fastidiosos divites dimittens inanes.

V. Panem de caelo praestitisti eis.
>R. Omne delectamentum in se habentem.

Oremus.

Deus, qui nobis
>sub sacramento mirabili Passionis tuae
>>memoriam reliquisti,

To the Most Holy Sacrament

O sacred banquet at which
    Christ is consumed,
    the memory of His Passion recalled,
    our soul filled with grace,
    and our pledge of future glory received!

How delightful, Lord, is Your spirit,
    which shows Your sweetness to men,
    offers the precious bread of heaven,
    fills the hungry with good things,
    and drives away all vain and loathsome things.

V. You have given them bread from heaven.
    R. A bread having all sweetness within it.

Let us pray.

God, Who left for us
    a memorial of Your Passion
       in this miraculous sacrament,

tribue, quaesumus,
      ita nos Corporis et Sanguinis tui
      sacra mysteria venerari,
          ut redemptionis tuae fructum in nobis
          jugiter sentiamus.

Qui vivis et regnas in saecula saeculorum.

          Amen

Grant, we implore You,
    that we may venerate
    the holy mystery of Your Body and Blood,
        so that we may ever experience in ourselves
        the fruitfulness of Your redemption.

You Who live and reign, world without end.

Amen

In Elevatione Corporis Christi

O salutaris hostia,
Quae caeli pandis ostium,
Bella premunt hostilia.
Da robur, fer auxilium.

In elevatione Corporis Christi,
consueverat dicere cum magna devotione et lacrymis:

Tu rex gloriae, Christe.
Tu Patris sempiternus es Filius.

Tu, ad liberandum suscepturus hominem,
non horruisti Virginis uterum.

Tu, devicto mortis aculeo,
aperuisti credentibus regna caelorum.

Tu ad dexteram Dei sedes
in gloria Patris.

Judex crederis esse venturus.

At the Elevation of the Body of Christ

> O Sacrifice for our salvation,
> Who Gate of Heaven opens wide,
> Our enemies press hard around us.
> Assist us strongly, be our guide.

*At the elevation of the Body of Christ, St. Thomas
was accustomed to say with great devotion and tears:*

You are Christ, the King of Glory.
> You are the Son, coeternal with the Father.

To liberate mankind,
> You did not disdain to enter a Virgin's womb.

Having conquered the sting of death,
> You opened heavenly realms to the faithful.

You sit at the right hand of God
> in the glory of the Father.

We believe
> You are the judge Who is to come.

Te ergo quaesumus tuis famulis subveni,
  quos pretioso sanguine redemisti.

Aeterna fac cum Sanctis tuis in gloria numerari.

Salvum fac populum tuum, Domine,
  et benedic hereditati tuae.

Et rege eos, et extolle illos usque in aeternum.

Per singulos dies benedicimus te.
  Et laudamus nomen tuum in saeculum
    et in saeculum saeculi.

Dignare, Domine, die isto sine peccato nos custodire.
  Miserere nostri, Domine, miserere nostri.

Fiat misericordia tua, Domine, super nos,
  quemadmodum speravimus in te.

In te, Domine, speravi;
  non confundar in aeternum.

Amen

Therefore, we ask You
    to come to the aid of Your servants
        redeemed by Your precious blood.

Include us among Your saints in eternal glory.

Bring salvation to Your people, Lord,
    and bless them as Your heirs.

Govern them and lead them into eternity.

Day after day we bless You.
    We praise Your name now and forever.

Lord, preserve us this day from sin.
    Have mercy upon us, Lord, have mercy.

Grant us Your mercy, Lord,
    even as we have placed our hope in You.

In You, Lord, have I trusted;
    let me not be confounded in eternity.

Amen

Adoro Te Devote, Latens Deitas

Sequentes versus etiam composuit, et dicebat,
quando levabatur Hostia in altari:

Adoro te devote, latens Deitas,
Quae sub his figuris vere latitas.
Tibi se cor meum totum subicit
Quia te contemplans totum deficit.

Visus, tactus, gustus, in te fallitur;
Sed auditu solo tuto creditur.
Credo quidquid dixit Dei Filius.
Nil hoc verbo veritatis verius.

In cruce latebat sola Deitas;
At hic latet simul et humanitas.
Ambo tamen credens atque confitens
Peto quod petivit latro poenitens.

Plagas, sicut Thomas, non intueor,
Deum tamen meum te confiteor;
Fac me tibi semper magis credere,
In te spem habere, te diligere.

Devoutly I Adore You, Hidden Deity

*St. Thomas was accustomed to pray the following verses
while he elevated the host at the altar.*

Devoutly I adore You, hidden Deity,
Under these appearances concealed.
To You my heart surrenders self
For, seeing You, all else must yield.

Sight and touch and taste here fail;
Hearing only can be believed.
I trust what God's own Son has said.
Truth from truth is best received.

Divinity, on the Cross, was hid;
Humanity here comes not to thought.
Believing and confessing both,
I seek out what the Good Thief sought.

I see no wounds, as Thomas did,
But I profess You God above.
Draw me deeply into faith,
Into Your hope, into Your love.

O memoriale mortis Domini,
Panis vivus, vitam praestans homini,
Praesta meae menti de te vivere
Et te illi semper dulce sapere.

Pie pelicane, Jesu Domine,
Me immundum munda tuo Sanguine,
Cujus una stilla salvum facere
Totum mundum quit ab omni scelere.

Jesu, quem velatum nunc aspicio,
Oro fiat illud, quod tam sitio,
Ut te revelata cernens facie,
Visu sim beatus tuae gloriae.

Amen

O memorial of the Lord's sad death,
Show life to man, O living Bread.
Grant that my soul may live through You,
By Your sweet savor ever fed.

Jesus Lord, my Pelican devout,
With Your Blood my sins dismiss.
One single drop could surely save
From sin this world's dark edifice.

Jesus, Whom now I see enveiled,
What I desire, when will it be?
Beholding Your fair face revealed,
Your glory shall I be blessed to see.

Amen

Ante Communionem

Omnipotens sempiterne Deus,
> ecce,
accedo ad sacramentum
>> unigeniti Filii tui
>>> Domini nostri Jesu Christi.

Accedo tanquam infirmus
>> ad medicum vitae,
> immundus
>> ad fontem misericordiae,
> caecus
>> ad lumen claritatis aeternae,
> pauper et egenus
>> ad Dominum caeli et terrae.

Rogo ergo
> immensae largitatis tuae abundantiam
quatenus meam
> curare digneris infirmitatem,
> lavare foeditatem,
> illuminare caecitatem,

Before Communion

All-powerful and everlasting God,
      behold,
I approach the sacrament
        of Your only-begotten Son,
           our Lord Jesus Christ.

As one infirm, I approach
      the balm of life,
    as one begrimed
      the fountain of mercy,
    as one blind
      the light of eternal splendor,
    as one poor and needy
      the Lord of heaven and earth.

Therefore, I ask that from the abundance
      of Your immense generosity
You may bestow that which is needed
    to cure my illness,
    to wash away my uncleanness,
    to illuminate my blindness,

ditare paupertatem,
vestire nuditatem,

ut panem Angelorum,
Regem regum,
et Dominum dominantium
tanta suscipiam reverentia et humilitate,
tanta contritione et devotione,
tanta puritate et fide,
tali proposito et intentione,
sicut expedit saluti
animae meae.

Da mihi, quaeso,
dominici Corporis et Sanguinis
non solum suscipere sacramentum,
sed etiam
rem et virtutem sacramenti.

O mitissime Deus,
da mihi
corpus unigeniti Filii tui
Domini nostri Jesu Christi,
quod traxit de Virgine Maria,

to enrich my poverty,
and to clothe my nakedness.

I ask all of this so that I might receive
    the Bread of Angels,
    the King of Kings,
    the Lord of Lords,
with that reverence and humility,
with that contrition and devotion,
with that purity and faith,
with that resolve and intention
    which is expedient
        for the salvation of my soul.

Allow me, I plead,
    to receive not only
        the sacrament of Your Body and Blood
    but also
        the reality and power of this sacrament.

O most gentle God,
    allow me to receive
        the Body of Your only begotten Son,
            our Lord Jesus Christ,
            Who was born of the Virgin Mary

sic suscipere
   ut corpori suo mystico merear incorporari
   et inter ejus membra connumerari.

O amantissime Pater,
  concede mihi
    dilectum Filium tuum,
      quem nunc velatum in via
        suscipere propono,
      revelata tandem facie
        perpetuo contemplari.

    Qui tecum vivit et regnat
    in unitate Spiritus Sancti Deus
    per omnia saecula saeculorum.

    Amen

so that I might be worthy
>to be united with His Mystical Body
>and counted among His members.

O most loving Father,
>give to me
>>Your beloved Son,
>>>Whom now I intend to receive
>>>>in this hidden form
>>>but hope to contemplate
>>>>face to face for all eternity,

>>Who with You lives and reigns
>>in the unity of the Holy Spirit,
>>world without end.

Amen

Post Communionem

Sit, Jesu dulcissime,
   sacratissimum Corpus tuum et Sanguis,
      dulcedo et suavitas animae meae,
      salus et robur
                  in omni tentatione,
      gaudium et pax
                  in omni tribulatione,
      lumen et virtus
                  in omni verbo et operatione,
      et finalis tutela in morte.

Amen

Short Prayer after Communion

Sweetest Jesus,
  Body and Blood most holy,
      be the delight and pleasure of my soul,
      my strength and salvation
              in all temptations,
      my joy and peace
              in every trial,
      my light and guide
              in every word and deed,
      and my final protection in death.

Amen

Altera Post Communionem

Gratias tibi ago,
      Domine sancte,
      Pater omnipotens,
      aeterne Deus,

qui me peccatorem, indignum famulum tuum,
  nullis meis meritis,
     sed sola dignatione
       misericordiae tuae,
       satiare dignatus es
          pretioso Corpore et Sanguine Filii tui
          Domini nostri Jesu Christi.

Et precor te ut haec sancta communio
     non sit mihi reatus ad poenam,
       sed intercessio salutaris ad veniam.

Sit mihi
    armatura fidei
    et scutum bonae voluntatis.

Longer Prayer after Communion

I give thanks to You,
        Holy Lord,
        Father almighty,
        everlasting God.

Not through any merit of my own,
   but only through the goodness of Your mercy,
      You have considered me
        — a sinner, a useless servant —
      worthy to be nourished
         with the precious Body and Blood
          of Your Son, our Lord Jesus Christ.

I pray to You that this Holy Communion
      will not condemn me to punishment
        but will rather secure my forgiveness.

May it be
     an armor of faith
     and a shield of good will.

Sit vitiorum meorum
    evacuatio;
        caritatis
        et patientiae,
        humilitatis
        et obedientiae,
        omniumque virtutum
    augmentatio;

contra insidias inimicorum omnium,
    tam visibilium quam invisibilium,
        firma defensio;

motuum meorum,
    tam carnalium quam spiritualium,
        perfecta quietatio;

in te uno ac vero Deo
    firma adhaesio;

atque finis mei felix consummatio.

Et precor te, ut ad illud ineffabile convivium
    me peccatorem perducere digneris,

May it
        remove my vices
        and increase in me
                charity,
                patience,
                humility,
                obedience,
                and all virtues.

May it be a firm defense
        against the plots of all my enemies,
                seen and unseen.

May it perfectly quiet my passions,
                physical and spiritual.

May it be the firmest bond to You,
                the one and true God.

May it give me final happiness.

I also pray that You bring me,
    a sinner,
        to that ineffable banquet where You dwell

ubi tu cum Filio tuo
et Spiritu Sancto.

Sanctis tuis es
lux vera,
satietas plena,
gaudium sempiternum,
jucunditas consummata,
et felicitas perfecta.

Per eundem
Christum Dominum nostrum.

Amen

with Your Son
and Holy Spirit.

You Who are for Your saints
        true light,
        complete fulfillment,
        eternal joy,
        consummate delight,
        and perfect happiness.

Through
the same Christ our Lord.

Amen

Hymns
from the
*Office of the
Feast of Corpus Christi*

Pange, Lingua, Gloriosi

Pange, lingua, gloriosi
Corporis mysterium
Sanguinisque pretiosi,
Quem in mundi pretium,
Fructus ventris generosi,
Rex effudit gentium.

Nobis datus, nobis natus
Ex intacta Virgine,
Et in mundo conversatus,
Sparso verbi semine
Sui moras incolatus
Miro clausit ordine.

In supremae nocte coenae
Recumbens cum fratribus,
Observata lege plene
Cibis in legalibus,
Cibum turbae duodenae
Se dat suis manibus.

Acclaim, My Tongue, This Mystery

Acclaim, my tongue, this mystery
Of glorious Body and precious Blood
Which the King of nations shed for us
A noble womb's sole fruitful bud.

Given and born from a Virgin pure,
Having made this world His dwelling place,
When the seeds of His words were sown afar
He ended His stay in wondrous grace.

With brethren reclining at that last meal,
He observes in full what the Law demands,
Then gives Himself as food instead
To apostles twelve with His own hands.

Verbum caro panem verum
Verbo carnem efficit;
Fit sanguis Christi merum.
Et si sensus deficit,
Ad firmandum cor sincerum
Sola fides sufficit.

Tantum ergo sacramentum
Veneremur cernui.
Et antiquum documentum
Novo cedat ritui.
Praestet fides supplementum
Sensuum defectui.

Genitori genitoque
Laus et jubilatio,
Salus, honor, virtus quoque
Sit et benedictio.
Procedenti ab utroque
Compar sit laudatio.

Amen

The Word in flesh makes true bread flesh,
The Blood of Christ then comes from wine.
Though senses fail to see this truth,
Faith will make pure hearts incline.

So great a sacrament, therefore,
Let us revere while kneeling down.
Let old laws yield to this new rite.
Let faith, not sense, conviction ground.

Praise and jubilation to the Father;
Honor, virtue, blessing to the Son;
And to the One Who proceeds from both
In equal measure may praise be sung.

Amen

Sacris Solemniis Juncta Sint Gaudia

Sacris solemniis juncta sint gaudia,
Et ex praecordiis sonent praeconia.
Recedant vetera, nova sint omnia
Corda, voces et opera.

Noctis recolitur coena novissima,
Qua Christus creditur agnum et azyma
Dedisse fratribus juxta legitima
Priscis indulta patribus.

Post agnum typicum expletis epulis,
Corpus dominicum datum discipulis
Sic totum omnibus quod totum singulis
Ejus fatemur manibus.

Dedit fragilibus corporis ferculum,
Dedit et tristibus sanguinis poculum,
Dicens: Accipite quod trado vasculum,
Omnes ex eo bibite.

Let Joys Be Joined to Solemn Feasts

Let joys be joined to solemn feasts.
Let praises from the depths resound.
Let old things pass, make all things new.
Let heart and voice and works abound.

Recall that final evening meal
When Christ did offer lamb and bread
According to the ancient law
From patriarchs inherited:

The feast of the Paschal lamb now over,
The Body of the Lord was shared.
Thus everything, to all and each,
From His own hands was then declared.

To the weak He apportioned flesh.
To the mournful He gave His blood so dear.
He said: Accept this cup I give;
All drink what you find here.

Sic sacrificium istud instituit,
Cujus officium committi voluit
Solis presbyteris, quibus sic congruit,
Ut sumant et dent ceteris.

Panis angelicus fit panis hominum,
Dat panis caelicus figuris terminum.
O res mirabilis! manducat Dominum
Pauper, servus et humilis.

Te trina Deitas unaque poscimus:
Sic nos tu visita, sicut te colimus;
Per tuas semitas duc nos quo tendimus
Ad lucem quam inhabitas.

Amen

Thus, this sacrifice He founded,
An act He willed then to allow
To priests alone, for whom is fit
All others to nurture and endow.

May the Bread of Angels be bread of man.
May bread on high all prophecies outgrow.
O wondrous thing! God is consumed
By the poor, the servile, and the low.

You, threefold God and one, we pray:
Be present as we worship well.
Lead us on Your pathways
To live in glory where You dwell.

Amen

Verbum Supernum Prodiens

Verbum supernum prodiens,
Nec Patris linquens dexteram,
Ad opus suum exiens,
Venit ad vitae vesperam.

In mortem a discipulo
Suis tradendus aemulis,
Prius in vitae ferculo
Se tradidit discipulis,

Quibus sub bina specie
Carnem dedit et sanguinem,
Ut duplicis substantiae
Totum cibaret hominem.

Se nascens dedit socium,
Convescens in edulium;
Se moriens in pretium,
Se regnans dat in praemium.

The Word from Heaven Now Proceeding

The Word from heaven now proceeding,
His Father's right hand never leaving,
Advancing to His proper work,
Approached His life's final evening.

By His disciple unto death
And soon by foes to be betrayed,
But first as life's true sustenance
To apostles He Himself conveyed.

To them beneath a twofold guise
He Flesh and Blood distributed;
Thus in corporeal substances
The entire man He justly fed.

Being born, He became our friend.
At supper, He became our food.
Dying, He paid our ransom's price
And reigning, gives eternal good.

O salutaris hostia,
Quae caeli pandis ostium,
Bella premunt hostilia.
Da robur, fer auxilium.

Uni trinoque Domino
Sit sempiterna gloria,
Qui vitam sine termino
Nobis donet in patria.

Amen

O Sacrifice for our salvation,
Who Gate of Heaven opens wide,
Our enemies press hard around us.
Assist us strongly, be our guide.

To the One and Triune God,
Be glory and eternal praise.
May He grant us life forever
And to our home our souls upraise.

Amen

Lauda, Sion, Salvatorem

Lauda, Sion, Salvatorem.
Lauda ducem et pastorem
In hymnis et canticis.

Quantum potes, tantum aude,
Quia major omni laude.
Nec laudare sufficis.

Laudis thema specialis,
Panis vivus et vitalis,
Hodie proponitur,

Quem in sacrae mensa coenae
Turbae fratrum duodenae
Datum non ambigitur.

Sit laus plena, sit sonora;
Sit jucunda, sit decora
Mentis jubilatio.

Praise, O Sion, Your Redeemer

Praise, O Sion, your Redeemer.
Praise your Prince and Shepherd
With canticle and hymn.

Dare to praise Him as you can,
For He is greater than all praise.
Our brightest praises are but dim.

A theme of special praising now
— Life-giving Bread, the Bread of Life —
Is proclaimed this day.

This Bread at holy supper
To brethren twelve was portioned out.
Let none this truth betray.

Let praise be full, let praise resound,
Let joyful and harmonious be
Our souls' deep jubilation.

Dies enim solemnis agitur,
In qua mensae primae recolitur
Hujus institutio.

In hac mensa novi Regis
Novum pascha novae legis
Phase vetus terminat.

Vetustatem novitas,
Umbram fugat veritas,
Noctem lux eliminat.

Quod in coena Christus gessit,
Faciendum hoc expressit
In sui memoriam.

Docti sacri institutis,
Panem vinum in salutis
Consecramus hostiam.

Dogma datur Christianis,
Quod in carnem transit panis
Et vinum in sanguinem.

For we observe a solemn day;
We now recall this founding,
Our feast's first celebration.

At this supper of our new King,
The Paschal feast's new covenant
Has put the old to flight.

The old will flee from what is new
As shadows flee from truth
And day casts out the night.

What Christ enacted at that meal
We evermore should re-enact,
His memory to perpetuate.

By this sacred action taught,
The bread and wine for our salvation
As victim now we consecrate.

This truth to Christians is proclaimed:
That to flesh, bread is transformed,
And transformed to blood is wine.

Quod non capis, quod non vides,
Animosa firmat fides
Praeter rerum ordinem.

Sub diversis speciebus,
Signis tantum et non rebus,
Latent res eximiae.

Caro cibus, sanguis potus,
Manet tamen Christus totus
Sub utraque specie.

A sumente non concisus,
Non confractus, non divisus,
Integer assumitur.

Sumit unus, sumunt mille;
Quantum isti, tantum ille.
Nec sumptus consumitur.

Sumunt boni, sumunt mali;
Sorte tamen inaequali
Vitae vel interitus.

What you can neither grasp nor see,
A lively faith will yet affirm
Beyond this world's design.

Under different guises there
— Which act as signs, not things —
Wondrous matters are enshrined.

Flesh is food and blood is drink.
Christ, however, still remains
Fully in each kind.

Left entire for each partaker,
Neither broken nor divided,
He is received into the soul.

If one or multitudes consume,
However many, He still is one.
Consumed, He yet stays whole.

Whether good or evil men receive,
They have unequal destinies:
Eternal life or else perdition,

Mors est malis, vita bonis.
Vide paris sumptionis
Quam sit dispar exitus.

Fracto demum sacramento,
Ne vacilles; sed memento
Tantum esse sub fragmento
Quantum toto tegitur.

Nulla rei fit scissura.
Signi tantum fit fractura,
Qua nec status nec statura
Signati minuitur.

Ecce panis Angelorum,
Factus cibus viatorum,
Vere panis filiorum,
Non mittendus canibus.

In figuris praesignatur,
Cum Isaac immolatur,
Agnus paschae deputatur,
Datur manna patribus.

Death for the bad, life for the good.
See how similar acts can end
In opposite condition.

When the Host at last is broken
From all doubting be restrained:
As much remains in a single part
As the primal whole contained.

No actual thing is cut apart,
Breaking but a sign is gained.
State and stature undiminished,
The Signified is yet retained.

Behold the Bread of Angels,
As pilgrims' food inherited!
It is the Bread of all true heirs,
Not to lowly dogs outspread.

In prototypes it was foreshadowed:
When Isaac to sacrifice was led,
When Passover lambs were set aside
And manna to our fathers fed.

Bone pastor, panis vere,
Jesu nostri miserere,
Tu nos pasce, nos tuere,
Tu nos bona fac videre
In terra viventium.

Tu qui cuncta scis et vales,
Qui nos pascis hic mortales,
Tuos ibi commensales,
Coheredes et sodales
Fac sanctorum civium.

Amen

Good Shepherd, Bread of Truth,
Lord Jesus, show Your clemency.
May You feed us, may You guard us,
May You let us see good things
In our homeland eternally.

You Who know and do all things
Feed us, though still captive here.
Make us fellow-citizens,
Co-heirs, and friends of all the saints
In that City bright and clear.

Amen

A Last Prayer

In Articulo Mortis

Sumo te pretium
      redemptionis animae meae.
Sumo te
      viaticum peregrinationis meae,
pro cujus amore
      studui, vigilavi et laboravi et praedicavi et docui.

Nihil unquam contra te dixi.

Sed si quid dixi ignorans,
            nec sum pertinax in sensu meo.
Sed si quid male dixi, totum relinquo correctioni
            Ecclesiae Romanae.

Amen

A Prayer at the Time of Death

I receive You,
>   Price of my redemption.
I receive You,
>   Viaticum of my pilgrimage,
For love of Whom I have
>   studied, kept vigil, labored, preached, and taught.

Never have I said anything against You.

If I have, it was in ignorance,
>   and I do not persist in my ignorance.
If I have taught anything false, I leave correction
>   of it to the Roman Catholic Church.

Amen

BIOGRAPHICAL NOTE
St. Thomas Aquinas (1225?-1274)

Scholar *and* saint! Certainly it's a rare combination in our day, but St. Thomas Aquinas was both. He devoted his entire life to comprehending God's Revelation — through reason, contemplation, and prayer — and to living in conformity with the call of that Revelation.

Born in Naples, St. Thomas studied at Monte Cassino Abbey and the University of Naples. In 1244, against the wishes of his family, he entered the Dominican Order.

The Dominicans sent Thomas to the University of Paris to study with the Aristotelian scholar, Albert the Great. In 1252, Thomas began his teaching career. Through many formal academic disputations, through his preaching, and in over 100 written volumes, St. Thomas gave his reason unreservedly to the service of Christian Revelation. Relying heavily on the Greek philosopher Aristotle, Thomas showed that Christian faith is credible, defensible, and intelligible.

Moreover, St. Thomas's prodigious scholarship nurtured his own spiritual development. He prayed intensely and was known to suffer the terrible spiritual trials and sublime consolations of the true ascetic and contemplative.

St. Thomas died on March 7, 1274, at the age of fifty. He was canonized in 1323 and proclaimed a Doctor of the Universal Church in 1567. In his encyclical *Æterni Patris* (August 4, 1879), Pope Leo XIII called on all men to "restore the golden wisdom of St. Thomas and to spread it far and wide for the defense and beauty of the Catholic Faith, for the good of society, and for the advantage of all sciences."

Sophia Institute Press

Sophia Institute is a non-profit institution that seeks to restore man's knowledge of eternal truth, including man's knowledge of his own nature, his relation to other persons, and his relation to God.

Sophia Institute Press serves this end in a number of ways. It publishes translations of foreign works to make them accessible for the first time to English-speaking readers. It brings back into print many books that have long been out of print. And it publishes important new books that fulfill the ideals of Sophia Institute. These books afford readers a rich source of the enduring wisdom of mankind.

Sophia Institute Press makes high-quality books available to the general public by using advanced, cost-effective technology and by soliciting donations to subsidize general publishing costs.

Your generosity can help us publish works containing the enduring wisdom of the ages. Please send your tax-deductible contribution to the address noted below. Your questions, comments, and suggestions are also welcome.

For your free catalog, call:

Toll-free: 1-800-888-9344

or write:

Sophia Institute Press
Box 5284, Manchester, NH 03108

Sophia Institute is a tax-exempt institution
as defined by the Internal Revenue Code, Section 501(c)(3).
Tax I.D. 22-2548708